D

ls

Renewals
01159 293388

THE LONDON BOROUGH
www.bromley.gov.uk

Please return/renew this item
by the last date shown.
Books may also be renewed by
phone and Internet.

D1331657

Raintree is an imprint of Capstone Global Library Limited, a company incorporated in England and Wales having its registered office at 7 Pilgrim Street, London, EC4V 6LB Registered company number: 6695582

www.raintreepublishers.co.uk
myorders@raintreepublishers.co.uk

Text © Capstone Global Library Limited 2014
First published in hardback in 2014
Paperback edition first published in 2015
The moral rights of the proprietor have been asserted.

Edited by Abby Colich, Dan Nunn, and Catherine Veitch
Designed by Marcus Bell
Picture research by Tracy Cummins
Production by Victoria Fitzgerald
Originated by Capstone Global Library Ltd
Printed and bound in China

ISBN 978 1 4062 6333 6 (hardback)
17 16 15 14 13
10 9 8 7 6 5 4 3 2 1

ISBN 978 1 4062 6341 1 (paperback)
18 17 16 15 14
10 9 8 7 6 5 4 3 2 1

British Library Cataloguing in Publication Data
Colich, Abby.
Paper. – (Exploring materials)
620.1'97-dc23
A full catalogue record for this book is available from the British Library.

Acknowledgements
The author and publisher are grateful to the following for permission to reproduce copyright material: Corbis p. 11 (© Imaginechina); Getty Images pp. 4 (© Bonita Cooke), 8 (© moodboard), 10, 23c (© Dev Carr), 15, 23a (© Lonely Planet), 19 (© Alistair Berg); Istockphoto p. 7 (© ei); Photo Researchers, Inc pp. 9 inset, 23b (© Tommaso Guicciardini); Shutterstock pp. 5 (© Subbotina Anna), 6a (© luchunyu), 6b (© Daniel Korzeniewski), 6c (© Ruth Black), 6d (© modd), 12 (© kotomiti), 13 (© AISPIX by Image Source), 14 (© Anatoliy Samara), 16 (© Zulhazmi Zabri), 17 (© Juriah Mosin), 18 (© Fer Gregory), 20 (© oznyakov), 22 (© Marcie Fowler - Shining Hope Images, © photobank.ch, © Elena Schweitzer); Superstock pp. 9, 23b (© John Zoiner/age fotostock), 21 (© age fotostock).

Front cover photograph of a boy holding cut-out figures reproduced with permission of Superstock (© Juice Images).

Back cover photograph reproduced with permission of Shutterstock (© kotomiti).

We would like to thank Valarie Akerson, Nancy Harris, Dee Reid, and Diana Bentley for their assistance in the preparation of this book.

Every effort has been made to contact copyright holders of material reproduced in this book. Any omissions will be rectified in subsequent printings if notice is given to the publisher.

Contents

What is paper?

Paper is a material.

Materials are what things are made from.

We use paper to make many different things.

Paper has many uses.

Where does paper come from?

Paper comes from trees or other plants.

pulp

Wood is cut up and made into a pulp. The pulp is made into paper.

Paper can be recycled or reused.

Recycled paper can be used to make new things.

What is paper like?

Paper can be different colours.

thin

thick

Paper can be thin or thick.
Thick paper is called card.

Paper can be cut and folded.

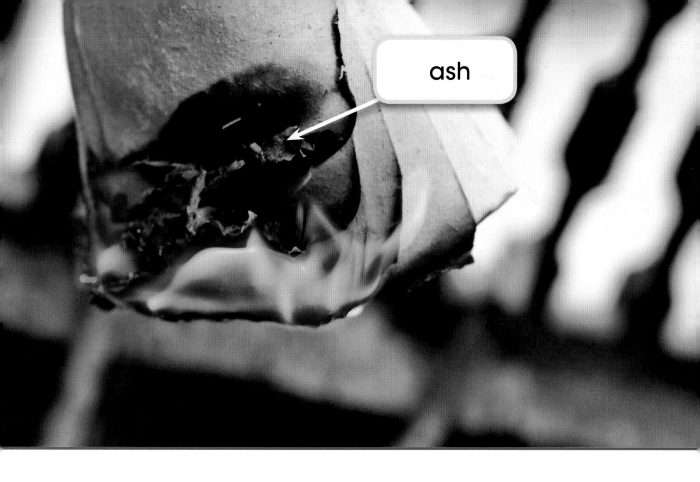

ash

Paper can burn and turn into ash.

How do we use paper?

We use paper to share stories.

We use paper to write letters.

We use paper to wrap food
and drink.

We use paper to store and carry things.

We use paper to paint on.

We use paper to blow our noses!

Quiz

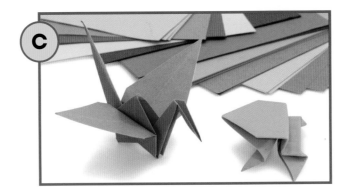

Which of these things are made of paper?

Answer on page 24.

Picture glossary

 **ash** grey powder left behind after something is burnt. Burnt paper turns into ash.

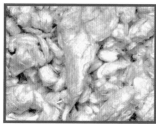 **pulp** mixture of ground-up wood and water

 **recycle** make used items into new things

Index

The **tissue paper (a)** and **coloured paper (c)** are made of paper.

Notes for parents and teachers

Before reading

Ask children if they have heard the term "material" and what they think it means. Reinforce the concept of materials. Explain that all objects are made from different materials. A material is something that takes up space and can be used to make other things. Ask children to give examples of different materials. These may include glass, plastic, and paper.

To get children interested in the topic, ask if they know what paper is. Identify any misconceptions they may have. Ask them to think about whether their ideas might change as the book is read.

After reading

- Check to see if any of the identified misconceptions have changed.
- Show the children examples of paper, including newspapers, books, and cardboard.
- Pass the paper objects round the children. Ask them to describe the properties of each item. Is the paper heavy or light? Is it thick or thin? Can it bend and fold? Ask them to name other items made from paper.